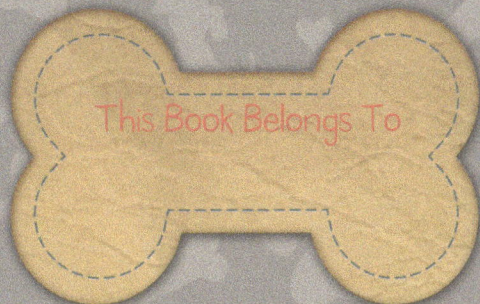
This Book Belongs To

Hero to the Rescue

The Memoir of an Unlikely Hero

by Heddie Wittlin-Leger

Author: Heddie Wittlin-Leger
Cover and Layout Designer: Jennifer Tipton Cappoen
Editor: Lynn Bemer Coble

Hero's Books is an imprint of **Paws and Claws Publishing, LLC.**
1589 Skeet Club Road, Suite 102-175
High Point, NC 27265
www.PawsandClawsPublishing.com
info@pawsandclawspublishing.com

ISBN #978-0-9906067-3-4
Printed in the United States

Dedication

Lovingly dedicated to my beloved
grandchildren Gabriel and Naomi.

"Be strong and courageous. Do not be afraid; do
not be discouraged, for the LORD your God will be
with you wherever you go."—*Joshua 1:9*

This is the story about Hero and the many lives that this people-loving, calm, supportive, compassionate, big black Rottweiler—known as a gentle giant—has touched and changed forever. Hero's legacy will never be forgotten.

Table of Contents

The purposes of this book are threefold:

1. To help people learn that puppies can be taught at a young age successfully.

2. To teach people that Rottweilers are great dogs, but must be trained properly, just like any other dog. Socialization and communication make all the difference with any dog. It is up to the human to help the dog learn proper social behavior around other humans and dogs. Any dog that demonstrates antisocial behavior or inappropriate behavior needs proper education regarding interactions to help him or her learn proper behaviors.

3. To help people understand that *cancer doesn't always mean the end of life, but can be a new way of living.* It means that we all have challenges of some kind, whether they are health-related or otherwise. The way that we live, what we do with our lives, and our quality of life are what matter most. Also cancer can be survived for varying lengths of time. Doctors can guess how long a person or an animal fighting cancer may be able to survive, but doctors can be mistaken. Cancer can and does go into remission. For different people and animals struggling with various forms of cancer, time spent in remission can vary widely. It's what happens during that remaining time that really counts, not how long the remission time lasts.

A Special Note From the Author

Dear reader,

It is my desire that you can see the main themes of this book as *courage in the face of adversity* and as *survival*, no matter what life throws at us. None of us are exempt from challenges in life. However, it is how we manage to deal with those challenges that makes all the difference in our quality of life. I am very passionate about being the conduit of hope and encouragement, for children of all ages, through this story and others that will follow through the years. This is the way Hero lived his short life and showed me by both his actions and interactions how to be that encourager, time and time again, through the many experiences we shared.

Each of us adults still lives with that child within us as we pass through the stages of the cycle of life. Messages of hope, inspiration, survival, and encouragement like the ones in this book are always relevant, no matter what our chronological age.

Hero never failed to offer hope, encouragement, support, comfort, and inspiration. He did this for and with everyone he influenced in his all-too-short life. He loved people and being with people, especially children. Hero was a real touchstone for me. In each and every situation, he always reminded me what courage and never giving up are all about. I'll never forget our gentle-giant, people-loving teddy bear of a dog. He lives on in my heart and in the spirit in which he lived life.

Many blessings to you and yours,
Heddie

Acknowledgments

My deepest, heartfelt gratitude and appreciation go first to my family. My husband Ron, for supporting me always. I also appreciate Ron for tolerating all of my evening outings to visit and my travel that took me away from home on many weekends in service with my companion Hero as we provided Animal-Assisted Interventions. Our daughters, Corrie and Traci, for being my inspiration in life. They are always questioning me and providing wonderful memories in our journeys with our myriad of pets. Our 4H family who formed the first ReCHAI (Research Center for Human-Animal Interaction) visiting team that visited at New Mark Assisted Living Center. Dr. Rebecca A. Johnson at the University of Missouri for her unwavering encouragement and direction throughout the years.

Special thanks to a long-standing friend, Nicole Shumate—founder of Paws & Effect™, who always aspires to the highest level of commitment and support and continually challenges me to higher ground.

Loving, caring, and compassionate Debbie Coon, the owner-breeder of Double D Rottweilers. She cared a great deal about sweet Hero and wanted to see him happy and successful.

Special thanks to Hero's first family: Dr. and Mrs. Carol Foster, and all of their extended family for their role in raising Hero, taking him with them everywhere, and training him as a puppy.

Dr. Joe Howard and the wonderful staff at Crossroads Animal Hospital who gave life to Hero as a puppy. They continued to provide loving care, encouragement, and support to Hero during our travels to and from the 25 weeks of chemotherapy treatments at the University of Missouri-Veterinary Medical Teaching Hospital.

The ever-caring staff at the University of Missouri-Veterinary Medical Teaching Hospital, especially the veterinary technicians who so lovingly administered chemotherapy to Hero.

My dear, long-standing friend and animal lover, Joan Arth, for getting us started in Liberty Public Schools with a long tradition of R.E.A.D.® programs for children in the Library.

Mid-Continent Public Library and Kansas City Public-School Media Centers for their continued support of R.E.A.D.® programs for children that utilize volunteers on registered animal-and-human therapy teams. These programs continue to thrive throughout the United States and far beyond.

Hero's and my faithful forever friends, Dana Marsh and her lovely Schnauzer, Megan, for their always-faithful partnership in R.E.A.D.® programs in schools and for their loving support during Hero's treatments. Patty Levine for many shared memories with Cheri and Hero, and Hallie Pals for her unwavering support in setting up programs in Grain Valley Public Schools even in the face of adversity.

Mo-Kan Pet Partners for their continued and ongoing development of animal-assisted therapy in Missouri and Kansas.

Lory Mayotte for her unwavering support, hard work, and caring heart.

It goes without saying that my life has been enriched by the memories created during our journey with Hero and all the wonderful animals that provide animal-assisted interventions, therapy, and reading instruction. All of those precious memories will live forever.

This book could not be possible without all of you and the caring guidance of Paws and Claws Publishing, LLC; Jennifer Tipton Cappoen; and Lynn Bemer Coble.

Much love and many thanks to all.   ~Heddie

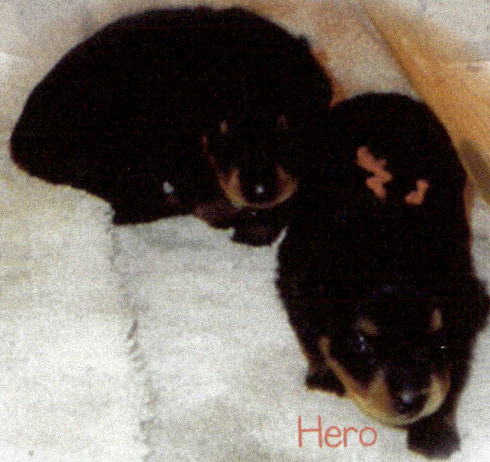

Hero

Hero at three weeks of age

Hero was not breathing when he was born on March 4, 2002. Dr. Joe Howard, the veterinarian, did puppy CPR on Hero immediately and revived him. Then the puppy could breathe on his own.

The vet named the puppy Hero. The doctor believed that Hero's life had been spared for an important reason. Dr. Howard had no idea how very true that belief would turn out to be.

Hero was like all puppies when they are little. He was very cute. However, …

Hero at six weeks of age with his Rottweiler Aunt T.J. at home with his first owners Dr. and Mrs. Foster

Puppies don't stay small for very long. Hero lived with two very nice people named Dr. and Mrs. Foster and his Rottweiler Aunt T.J.

Hero's Aunt T.J. was about eight or nine years old when the Fosters got Hero as a puppy. They had wanted another Rottweiler, because they knew T.J. was getting older. They didn't want to wait until she died and then be without a dog.

Hero was such a calm puppy that the breeder, Debbie Coon at Double D Rottweilers, thought it would be a great match. She was right. It was.

Hero really loved Mrs. Foster very much.

Hero was very smart and liked learning new things. He learned manners at a very young age. Most puppies can learn commands like Sit, Down, and Stay when they're young. They can also learn to come to their owners *(recall)*, walk well on a leash, meet people and other dogs politely, ride in a car well, watch their owners, and wait at a given door or at a different location.

He learned his lessons by using *clicker training*. Clicker training is a positive way to teach dogs. The clicker's clicking sound tells dogs that they have done something good and that a reward is coming.

For any pet, learning new things can be like putting a puzzle together. With clicker training, the puzzle pieces seem to fit together better and more easily.

One day Hero's owner, Mrs. Foster, became very ill. She had cancer. She didn't want to die and leave her Hero.

The gentle big black dog stayed right by her side throughout her whole fight with cancer. He refused to leave her alone. His was truly unconditional love.

He knew that she needed him and his strength, support, and presence. Hero helped keep Mrs. Foster alive longer than anyone had expected.

A very sad day for Hero

Unfortunately, Hero's owner, Mrs. Foster, died. Dr. Foster decided that he couldn't keep Hero and T.J. anymore.

T.J. went to another home.

Hero needed to find a new home. Dr. Foster packed the big black dog's bags. Everyone who knew Hero started looking for a new home for him.

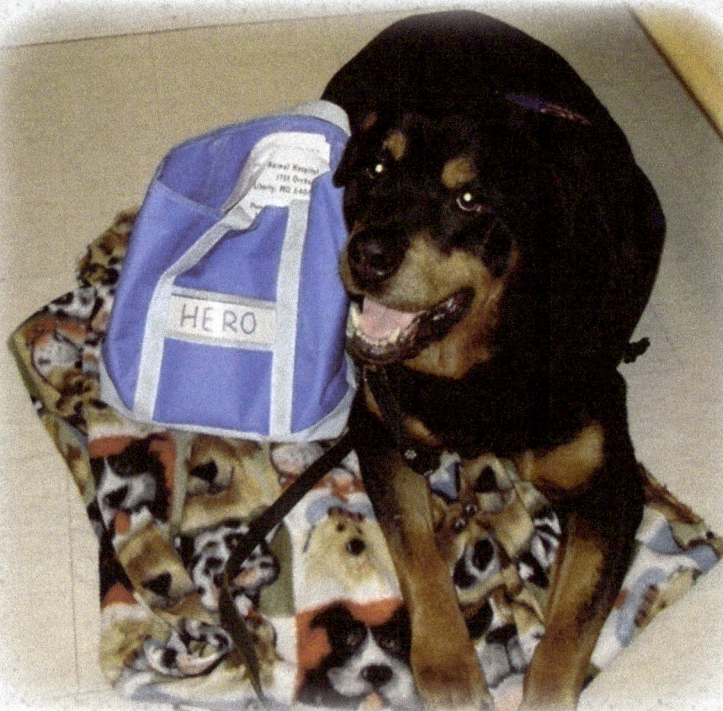

They looked and looked and looked. Hero stayed hopeful during the search for his new home. But he missed Mrs. Foster so much.

Hero was sent back to the Double D Rottweilers kennel and the breeder, Debbie Coon. She didn't know what to do with the sad big black dog. He missed his human family so much that he spent his time sitting outdoors on the concrete run—even in Missouri's wintry ice, cold, and snow—even though it was a very nice place with heated indoor kennels. Hero was waiting for his family to return for him. Sometimes it was so cold that his skin would freeze to the concrete. He was a very loyal dog.

Poor Hero lived in Debbie's kennel for about six months. Even though Hero knew all of the dogs in the kennel well, he was still sad there.

Dr. Foster and the breeder asked all of the big black dog's friends to help him find a new home. Hero had tons of friends because of all of his former owners' family members, the local business owners who knew Dr. Foster well, his veterinarian and the vet's staff, the dog-show people, and more. There were so many people who cared about Hero and were trying their hardest to find a new home for the gentle, big black dog.

It is really, really hard for big black adult dogs to find homes. Lots of people just don't seem to like them. The months dragged on for Hero.

To make things even more difficult, many people think that Rottweilers are bad dogs. People are often afraid of Rottweilers.

Hero just couldn't understand why no one wanted to love him, receive his love, and give him a home. All he wanted was a new home and a new family.

Those were several very long months in Debbie's kennel at Double D Rottweilers.

But Hero's luck was about to change.

Hero was taken to visit a nice lady who lived in the country. She'd heard about the big black dog from a buddy at school. Her friend had told her that Mrs. Foster had died and that Hero needed a new home. The lady and her family already had several dogs and really did not want another dog.

The minute Hero walked into the Legers' living room, he sat down and made himself at home. All of the other dogs liked Hero almost immediately. Since he fit into their family so quickly, the Legers decided to keep Hero and adopted him.

At Dr. Joe Howard's Crossroads Animal Clinic, they threw a big party when they found out that Hero was going to get to stay in town and live with the Leger family. The vet was the one who had saved Hero at birth. He's a Christian man, and he said that he'd been praying for Hero to find a good home. His prayers had been answered in the best possible way.

*Hero's new
permanent home*

Hero was very happy in his new home. But he still missed his first owner very much. He was homesick. He had *separation anxiety*. He wanted to see Mrs. Foster again.

Hero's new owners knew that he would feel better if he had a job to do. He had such a gentle spirit. And he was so calm and confident. Hero first went to school to learn how to be a therapy dog. He then passed the therapy-dog evaluations for *four* different organizations.

Hero was registered with all of the following: Pet Partners International; Delta Society® Pet Partners®; ReCHAI (Research Center for Human-Animal Interaction); Pets for Life, Inc.; a local organization; and Therapy Dogs International (TDI).

Hero was certified by Dog Scouts of America™. This is a very difficult certification for a dog to earn. You can read more about this on page 68 of this book.

Hero also earned his Canine Good Citizen certification from the American Kennel Club. He had other titles as well.

Heddie wanted to put people at ease as much as possible. That's why she got so many credentials for Hero. She wanted people to trust him and not to fear him.

Pet Partners®
Touching Lives, Improving Health

PETS FOR LIFE, INC.
Pets helping people

DELTA SOCIETY®
The Human–Animal Health Connection®
PET PARTNERS®

Research Center for
Human-Animal Interaction

Dog Scouts of America™
Dog Scouts
www.dogscouts.org

CANINE GOOD CITIZEN
An AMERICAN KENNEL CLUB Program

THERAPY DOGS INTERNATIONAL
PAWS AWHILE FOR LOVE

At therapy-dog school, Hero learned to be a really good listener.

He learned to sit quietly.

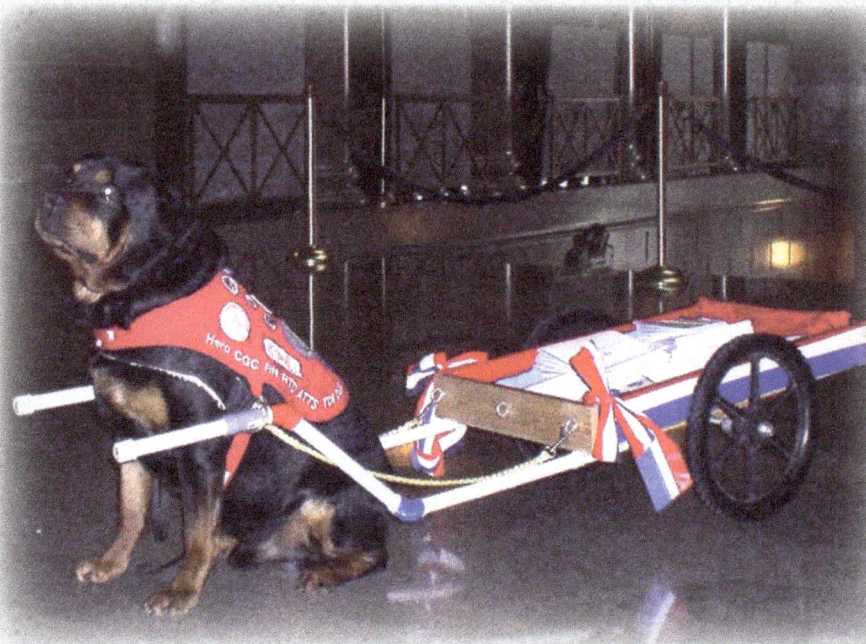

He also learned to be a good helper. Hero earned his
Carting badge from the Dog Scouts of America™. Later
he put it to good use in Parkersburg, Iowa, after their
devastating tornado. Hero used his cart to carry water
to residents in their homes and to workers helping with
cleanup.

Hero learned to be gentle, kind, and respectful.

Hero learned to be polite, to wait his turn, and never to push or shove.

Hero also learned to be a good sport and to get along well with others.

The most important thing of all that Hero learned was how to be a good friend.

Hero's new jobs and visits

Hero loved his new family and his important new job of being a therapy dog. He really enjoyed making people happy. He was good at it.

Hero loved visiting with children in schools and libraries. He couldn't get enough of them.

Above all else, he loved to make people smile. Oh, how he lived for those smiles.

Hero and Heddie visited hospitals and nursing homes too. Heddie always sensed that Hero was looking for Mrs. Foster, his first owner. He would enter every door slowly, peeking around the corner. He always seemed to be hoping to see Mrs. Foster just one more time.

Finally Heddie realized how exhausted Hero always was after those visits. She understood that the smells and equipment at the nursing homes and hospitals surely triggered those early memories. Hero had stayed right by Mrs. Foster's side through her entire illness.

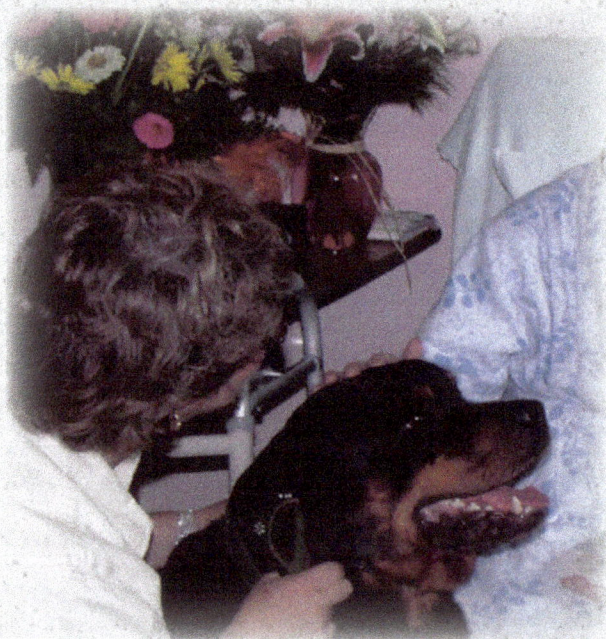

Local business owners liked Hero because he would come along with his owner to local events, parades, and business meetings. He went with Heddie to the Rotary Club, the Lions Club, and others. Owners of some stores invited Hero to be a guest visitor. The bookstore and local pet stores loved to have him come and visit. He was so dog neutral. And he was good with people of all ages.

The local fire department often asked Hero to do their pet-safety programs. He helped children and paramedics understand how to act around a dog a person didn't know. Hero was a demo dog for many different walks of life.

He also could pull a cart and gave children rides, which they loved. That made him an added attraction at events.

One day Hero did not feel well at all. He didn't want to eat. Over and over again, he looked at Heddie and then at his stomach. She was really worried about him. On April 27, 2010, Hero's owner took him to see Dr. Joe Howard. The veterinarian's blood tests didn't show anything seriously wrong for an older dog. Then the vet did X-rays of Hero's stomach and an ultrasound. They showed that Hero's spleen was larger than it should have been. The big black dog needed surgery to save his life.

On May 4, 2010, Dr. Joe did a *splenectomy* on Hero to remove his spleen. Later he diagnosed Hero with *splenic lymphosarcoma*. That was when Hero and Heddie found out that he had cancer in his spleen. Dr. Howard told them that Hero's spleen weighed eight pounds and was full of tumors. His spleen had been ready to burst at any time. The vet said it was a miracle that the spleen had not burst. If it had, Hero would have died instantly. Hero was very lucky.

That was the second miracle Dr. Howard had experienced with Hero. The first happened the day he was born.

Dr. Howard explained that *chemotherapy* to treat the cancer would be very expensive. He also said that treatment probably would not give Hero that much longer to live. The vet recommended not treating the cancer. However, Heddie disagreed. She tried to find someone local who could provide chemotherapy treatments. There was no one. Then she started to call and E-mail the university veterinary programs.

Hero, Dr. Joe Howard, and his staff

Heddie called her dear friend, Dr. Rebecca A. Johnson, at the University of Missouri ReCHAI (Research Center for Human-Animal Interaction) program. She asked Dr. Johnson if their veterinary center could help Hero. Dr. Johnson talked to the lead veterinarian. She found out that they were conducting a study that might help Hero.

It was probably due to Dr. Johnson's contact that they had Hero at their veterinary clinic that very week.

Hero's owner, Heddie, took him to the University of Missouri-Veterinary Medical Teaching Hospital in Columbia for cancer treatments. He was treated in the Veterinary Department. At that time, the university did not have an *oncology unit*. Now they have a separate, special unit for cancer patients.

During Hero's first visit there on May 12, 2010, the doctors told Heddie that Hero had *stage IV lymphosarcoma*. They found that the cancer had spread to his lymph nodes. Luckily it had not spread any farther. The veterinarians did surgery on Hero's *lymph nodes* to remove more cancerous nodes.

For 25 weeks, Heddie took Hero to the University of Missouri for chemotherapy treatments. She took vacation time from work for each trip. Ron wasn't able to go, because he had to work.

Before every chemotherapy treatment, the doctors had to check Hero's blood to make sure that he had gotten well from the last treatment. If he hadn't gotten well, they couldn't have given Hero the next treatment.

Dr. Joe Howard and Dr. Christy Wilkerson

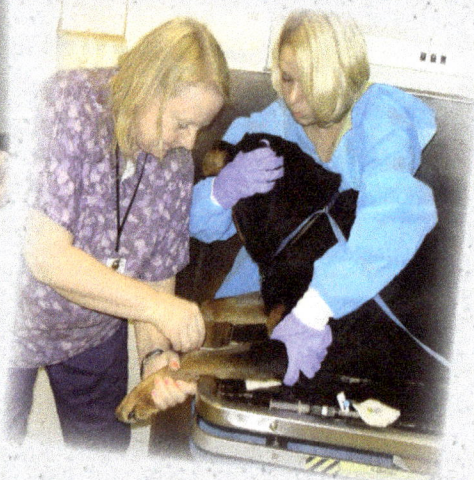

In the photo below, Vincristine—which is a chemotherapy drug—is being given directly into Hero's front leg.

One good thing for Hero was that the treatment program that he was in had a small risk of *side effects*.

Also as many as 80% to 90% of dogs that received this treatment went into *remission*. Dogs that went into remission usually stayed in remission for many months. That made the Legers and everyone who knew Hero hopeful.

Hero received great medical care at the University of Missouri. His treatment plan helped him heal.

Hero was very brave throughout the treatments. He knew that the veterinarians were doing their best to help him get better. Hero never gave up. The doctors' notes indicated how sweet Hero was during their examinations and treatments.

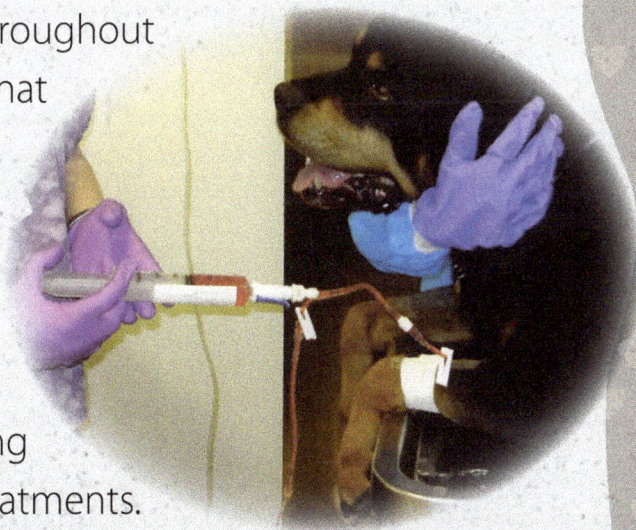

Hero was one of those lucky dogs. He went into remission. For over a year, Hero was in remission from the cancer. That's a long time, especially since he was an older dog. One year in a dog's life is equal to about seven years for a human.

During the time Hero remained in remission, he and Heddie visited children who were fighting cancer in several hospitals. Hero encouraged them. He helped them not to be afraid. He showed them how to survive, even when things didn't look good. He gave them support, love, and caring.

Hero still did all of his favorite things. He enjoyed all his friends every day. He enjoyed playing outdoors.

Hero still visited schools, libraries, and hospitals. He loved all of those visits so much. He loved being around all of the children. He loved seeing them smile.

Hero was still having lots of fun. He was in parades.

Heddie and Hero visited a Ronald McDonald House several times. They visited both the children undergoing treatment and their families. Their visits were therapeutic ones for everyone at the Ronald McDonald House, including the staff there. Sometimes people would pet Hero. At other times, Heddie and Hero played games with or read with the children.

The pair visited the Ronald McDonald House whenever they were requested to be there for special situations and families. One family requested Hero on a regular basis. They were from Arizona and missed their dog so much. Their little girl started to get better, and her attitude was lifted whenever Hero visited with her. Now she is a young woman graduating from school. She stayed friends with Hero even after going back home to Arizona.

Sometimes Heddie and Hero visited the Ronald McDonald House on Christmas Eve so that the people there would not feel so lonely on the holiday.

One day Hero wasn't doing at all well. He had vomited and had had really bad diarrhea all night the night before. Heddie and Ron didn't know why. By morning, Hero was dehydrated and very weak. Heddie knew that Hero wanted to see Dr. Joe Howard, his veterinarian, one last time.

Ron and Heddie carried Hero to his favorite place, the back of their Jeep. They took him straight to Dr. Joe Howard's clinic. The vet gave Hero a saline IV to *rehydrate* him. Heddie thought it was odd that the doctor gave the big black dog the IV in the back of the Jeep. All of the vet techs who knew Hero came out, hugged him, said they loved him, and told him good-bye.

Heddie still didn't see the signs of what was to come. She thought the IV fluids would help Hero get better. Now—after all these years—she thinks that Hero had wanted to go say good-bye to his good friend and to see him one last time.

The Legers drove Hero back home. As soon as they pulled into the driveway, Hero quietly passed away. Heddie saw him take his last breath and sat with him in the back of the Jeep. She honestly thought that they had more time, and she had never seen a dog die naturally before that day. It was calm and peaceful.

Hero had said his last good-byes, and he was ready. Heddie brought each of the other dogs out to see him and to say good-bye. This was a very sad day for all of them.

Ron and Heddie drove Hero to Rolling Acres Memorial Gardens and stayed with him for a while. The staff members were very kind, understanding, and compassionate. Then the staff there rolled Hero away. It was one of the saddest days of Heddie's life.

A friend had sent them a handmade, pot-shaped urn that was the exact likeness of Hero's face for his ashes.

He had survived longer than anyone had expected. He had lived the full life cycle. He had touched people in positive ways from the moment he was born. He left his body in the same way in a caring, nondramatic, very natural manner. He died peacefully in his favorite place in the back of the Jeep. The gentle, people-loving, big black dog died on his own from old age and health complications.

Hero had lived a good and full life. He had provided support, encouragement, caring, and love to many people. He will never be forgotten.

What Hero taught everyone he met

Hero lived his whole life in a manner that showed how we all should consider treating one another. One of unconditional love, kindness, and a nonjudgmental nature. He taught us to treat all living beings in such a manner that we improve their quality of life. He taught us not to pay attention to their race, color, or genetic or physical makeup. What Hero taught us makes the world a kinder, gentler place to live.

Hero lived this gentility, gave it to others, and in turn received it back many times over. We can learn much from this huge teddy bear of a dog that became a hero to so many.

The timeless gift of just being can never be replaced. For that he will always be remembered.

About the Author

Heddie is a city girl with a country heart. As a married adult, she has lived with her husband, Ron, for over 40 years in the country in Missouri on a hobby farm with various companion animals. They include chickens, ducks, geese, guinea pigs, cats, fish, birds, dogs, and horses. Their two grown daughters were never without chores to do. Heddie considers that part of the growing and learning experiences for children. Children exposed to the outdoors and fresh air and offered interactions with animals learn life skills that serve them well into their adult years and throughout their lives.

She spent 30 years in the educational family in the local public-school district, starting as a classroom aide and holding various positions along the way. Heddie's vision gave her the desire to begin a before- and after-school child-care program in their hometown before such programs were in vogue. Although her vision faced stiff opposition, the time-proven truth is that mothers—especially single mothers—and families with little or no support system needed this service and needed it then. Heddie's dream quickly grew into a thriving service caring for children not only before and after school, but also during summer months. The program still has a continual waiting list to this day.

Heddie will readily admit that crafts give her more stress than relaxation. Trying to crochet and knit—only to find items in knots—and losing count trying to make pretty cross-stitch fabric patterns cause her much duress. She tried her hand at quilting and couldn't sew a straight line, but with the help of a friend, she was able to complete quilts for her grandchildren. Heddie is best known for not being able to color or paint between the lines, and a local artist she took lessons from suggested that she take up another form of craft. She does love to sing and play the guitar, but only when no one is listening, except maybe the crickets and bullfrogs.

She found her place working with children and animals, through animal-assisted therapy and the Research Center for Human-Animal Interaction (ReCHAI). Her gifts and talents have been shared with thousands of children at schools, libraries, summer camps, special-needs programs, 4H, Girl and Boy Scouts, children's cancer wards in hospitals, and a myriad of other activities that involve children, including domestic-violence shelters. Hero was an integral part of their many interactions with all of the children and families that have been touched by their simple gifts of time and caring.

Currently Heddie is an instructor and evaluator for a therapy-animal organization. She also teaches offenders to train and socialize shelter dogs through Missouri Puppies for Parole. Her passion for helping others understand canine and animal behavior never wavers. As a Professional Humane Educator, her humane education classes are in high demand. Heddie's household remains one that has gone to the dogs, but also includes two cats, Cleo and Dove; a rescued racehorse, Celebrity Jamie (another story to be told); two mini horses; and a fish that loves to be hand-fed. Her husband, Ron, adores all the animals and agrees they add a zest to life that he didn't expect.

Her greatest joy in life is spending time with her grandchildren exploring everything about life from their perspectives. Their joy is infectious and their laughter contagious. We each have a bit of our childhood past in us, and grandchildren "re-awaken" that child within. It is one of the great blessings in life.

"Beginning with this moment,
treat every living being as if
it were their last moment.
Extend to all the kindness and
understanding you possess,
with no thought of anything in return.
Your life will change dramatically
in a positive manner."

Many blessings to you and yours,
Heddie Wittlin-Leger
ABCDT-L2, ADT, CDT, CHES, CPDT-KA
Owner of The Pawzone, Pet Care and Coaching
Founder of Hero's Hope Pet-Assist
www.thepawzone.com/heros_hope_pet-assist

Hero's Hope

Hero's Hope was formed in Hero's honor to help other dogs like him. Since forming Hero's Hope, organizers Heddie Leger, Dori Thomas, Sherry Edwards, Lory Mayotte, and Wendy Schindler have collaborated with the organization www.2milliondogs.org to bring a fundraiser to the city of Liberty, Missouri, in order to raise funds for cancer research for both animals and humans.

They have also raised funds to support Hero's Hope programs like Pet-Assist and Missouri Puppies for Parole. They've raised funds for various animal shelters, including the Liberty Animal Shelter, as well.

Hero's Hope Pet-Assist

Hero's Hope Pet-Assist was formed to help keep pets in their loving homes by supporting their families. The mission of Hero's Hope Pet-Assist is to help improve the quality of life including—but not limited to—assisting pet owners affected by the aging process, ill health, disability, being a veteran of war, or being in a crisis due to a financial or medical emergency, the loss of employment, and/or the loss of a home.

The goal of Hero's Hope Pet-Assist is to assist with food, daily care, or minor medical assistance so that the affected pet owner can keep their pet in their home. This organization promotes responsible pet ownership and upholds humane treatment of animals by providing educational materials when necessary.

Hero's Hope Pet-Assist is an all-volunteer charitable and educational nonprofit group based in the Midwest. Hero's Hope Pet-Assist is designed to keep pets in their homes.

Hero's Hope Pet-Assist also functions as a source of education and training for all aspects of humane, responsible pet ownership and pet care.

Hero's Hope Pet-Assist is designed with flexibility in mind with the ultimate goal of a smooth integration with animal shelters and rescues when necessary, especially in the event of an emergency or a disaster.

Hero's Hope Pet-Assist provides its services free of charge and relies solely on donations, grants, membership dues, and fundraisers to operate and conduct business.

You can find out more about Hero's Hope Pet-Assist at www.thepawzone.com/heros_hope_pet-assist.

You can find Hero's Hope Pet-Assist on Facebook at Hero's Hope.

Hero thanks each and every one of you for your kindness and generosity in helping these people and their pets in their times of need.

Missouri Puppies for Parole

Puppies for Parole sponsored by the Missouri Department of Corrections is important. Trainers participate on a regular basis, providing free training services in group settings at correctional facilities. There are currently many offender/handlers participating on a rotating basis in some capacity in select correctional facilities.

Dogs are carefully evaluated and selected from local-area animal shelters and then placed in the correctional facilities. With the guidance of the offender/handlers, the chosen dogs are expected to pass the CGC before being adopted out. They also are trained and evaluated on the Association of Professional Dog Trainers (APDT) C.L.A.S.S. (Canine Life and Social Skills) program. They are given an intense behavior assessment before they can be adopted by their new families.

This program also works with the Missouri Veterans Home, placing dogs in select facilities, in mental-health rehabilitation centers, and with carefully screened veterans who are individuals with physical or mental assistance needs. The current facilities served maintain a 99.9% adoption rate with very few returns.

Through the Puppies for Parole program, they have discovered a triple-crown winning situation in which all involved benefit. The local animal shelter, the correctional facility, and the resulting family that receives a well-trained dog all benefit from this training program.

The adventure of remolding and rehabilitating in a training program that identifies shelter dogs and places them with offender/handlers for training in correctional facilities never ends. There are unlimited opportunities for training in many different venues. Offender/handlers often provide advanced training to enable a selected dog to provide assistance services for veterans or those with physical or emotional needs that require the assistance of a trained dog through a partnership with ComTrea AP4P. Overall, in just five years, more than 3,500 dogs have graduated from the program and have been adopted.

Hero and his daughter Halo were the first demo dogs in the program in St. Joseph, Missouri, helping offender/handlers learn about safe and kind training methods to use with dogs. Halo's friend Candy was the first graduate of the program and was featured in an issue of *Metro Pet Magazine*.

No taxpayer money is spent on the Puppies for Parole program. Puppies for Parole uses no general revenue and operates solely on private donations and donations from offender organizations. The program also gets donations from Royal Canin pet food company.

To find out more about the Puppies for Parole program, please go to the following: www.doc.mo.gov

Hero's Last Hospital Visit In Remembrance

Here is my very last photo of Hero. He insisted on visiting a hospital. He wanted to go. I was going to let him stay in the car, but he didn't want to stay there. He wanted to visit his friends.

He was smiling at me with a really big smile, with his chest stuck out as if to say, "Look, Ma. Look at me. I am so happy."

Hero's Thanks to Everyone

🐾 Who helped him live.

🐾 Who helped him find a second home.

🐾 Who helped train him for a job and find a new purpose.

🐾 Who helped him visit at schools and libraries.

🐾 Who helped him earn his Dog Scouts of America™ certification.

🐾 Who helped him heal from cancer.

🐾 Who played with him and read to him.

🐾 Who helped him visit children with cancer at hospitals.

🐾 Who helped him visit people at nursing homes and hospitals.

🐾 Who helped his friends by giving them food and other assistance through Hero's Hope Pet-Assist.

Double D Rottweilers—Debbie and Don Coon's Legacy

Debbie and Don Coon are very well-known dog breeders in Missouri. They love Rottweilers. They had a really nice kennel and are very responsible breeders. *Responsible breeding* is critical due to the myriad of problems created by puppy mills and backyard breeders.

Their kennel was called Double D Rottweilers. Many of their dogs won high honors. All of the dogs in their kennel were relatives: brothers, sisters, mother, aunts, and uncles. The Double D Rottweiler line is recognized nationally for their wonderful temperament, health, and physical soundness. According to Heddie, they were "wonderful, lovely dogs."

Hero's grandmother, *Double D Matai,* was a Westminster Dog Show winner as a Select Champion. Hero's given registered name was *Double D American Hero.* The Double D line has produced many champions and Best of Breed winners.

Debbie and Don's kennel had one litter of puppies that Hero fathered before they knew he carried a gene for cancer. That litter was pretty famous, including an American Kennel Club Grand Champion named *Double D Keeper of the Keys,* better known for his call name of *Haggred.* It also included *Halo,* Hero's daughter, that went on to be much like Hero. She and Hero were the first demo dogs for the Missouri Puppies for Parole program, and Halo also did search-and-rescue work for the Clay-Platte Sheriff Department and the local official Community Emergency Response Team (CERT) organization. Her AKC registered name was *Double D Full Circle.*

Double D Rottweilers are well known as blue-ribbon winners both inside the show ring and in the "ring of life."

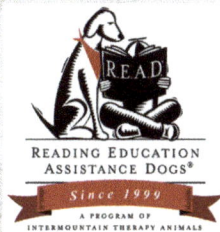

Reading Education Assistance Dogs®
(R.E.A.D.® Program)
A Program of Intermountain Therapy Animals

"The mission of the R.E.A.D.® program is to improve the literacy skills of children through the assistance of registered therapy teams as literacy mentors.

"The Reading Education Assistance Dogs® [R.E.A.D.®] program improves children's reading and communication skills by employing a powerful method: reading to a dog. But not just any dog. R.E.A.D.® dogs are registered therapy animals who volunteer with their owner/handlers as a team, going to schools, libraries and many other settings as reading companions for children.

"Today, thousands of registered R.E.A.D.® teams work throughout the United States and Canada. R.E.A.D.® is one of those ideas that, in the words of Bill Moyers, 'pierces the mundane to arrive at the marvelous.'

"Intermountain Therapy Animals, a nonprofit organization, launched R.E.A.D.® in 1999 as the first comprehensive literacy program built around the appealing idea of reading to dogs, and the program has been spreading rapidly and happily ever since!

"To find out more about teams in the Kansas City area, contact pawzone@yahoo.com or contact Intermountain Therapy Animals directly at info@therapyanimals.org."

The above is from the "About R.E.A.D.® and How to Become a R.E.A.D.® Team" web page on the Intermountain Therapy Animals website at the following: www.therapyanimals.org/R.E.A.D.html

Hero loved being part of this program for years. He and Heddie volunteered in countless schools, libraries, and other venues. They made an impact on many youngsters' lives. Librarians all over the Kansas City public school system knew Heddie and Hero and loved their involvement in the R.E.A.D.® events.

In the years to come, maybe volunteers in this vibrant and ever-growing literacy program will be reading this book and the other books written by Heddie Wittlin-Leger that will be coming in the future from Paws and Claws Publishing, LLC! All of Heddie's books will be inspiring for readers and listeners alike.

Paws & Effect™ Nonprofit Organization
"Take a moment. Make a difference."

Established in 2006, Paws & Effect™ is a Des Moines, Iowa-based 501(c)(3) nonprofit organization that raises, trains, and places service dogs with military veterans and children diagnosed with medical needs. The majority of their recipients include children with autism and combat veterans with Post-Traumatic Stress Disorder (PTSD), Traumatic Brain Injury (TBI), and/or mobility issues.

The group also registers therapy animals through Pet Partners. They provide Pet Partners for animal-assisted activities and animal-assisted therapy. Their Pet Partner programs include their Abilities Through Agility Program at Child*Serve*. This program integrates dog agility with physical, occupational, and speech therapy in a group environment. Ultimately, they're striving to expand this program to make it a future event at the Special Olympics.

They also have Pet Partner programs at facilities across the State of Iowa, including the following:

- Child*Serve*—They partner with families to help children with special health-care needs live a *great* life.
- Civic Center of Greater Des Moines Family Series and Iowa schools and libraries unite with P&E for our literacy programs.
- St. Luke's Hospital in Cedar Rapids

Paws & Effect™ regularly hosts NADAC-sanctioned dog-agility events for fun and fund-raising. These events also allow children already participating in their programs an opportunity to demonstrate their new skills by teaming with a Pet Partner during a run.

The new Paws & Effect™ Beaverdale neighborhood storefront also serves as a training center, as well as the home base to Troop 232 of the Dog Scouts of America™.

Paws & Effect™ was also an American Humane Association Charity Partner from 2010 to 2014. They were the winning Charity Partner in 2010 and 2014. In 2014, they won when the dog named Susie won the 2014 American Humane Association Hero

Dog Award™—the national honor. Earlier Susie had won the Therapy Dog category of the 2014 competition. Susie is the inspiration for Susie's Law in North Carolina; the inspiration for three children's books written by her adoptive owner, Donna Smith Lawrence, and published by Paws and Claws Publishing, LLC (the publishers of this book); the inspiration for the movie *Susie's Hope;* a part of the feature-length documentary *A Dog Named Gucci* by Director Gorman Bechard; and a participant in all speaking engagements in many elementary schools in North Carolina—through her and Donna's Susie's Hope™ nonprofit organization. The two teach children to be responsible pet owners, to be safe around unfamiliar animals, and ways to be animal-rights activists capable of making changes in state laws protecting animals, just like Donna, Susie, and Susie's Team did. "One animal and one person can make a difference in our world." Ironically, Lynn Bemer Coble (the editor of this book) helped Donna Smith Lawrence make the decision to pair Susie with Paws & Effect™ when she and Donna were completing Susie's application for the 2014 American Humane Association Hero Dog Award™ competition in February 2014. At that time, neither Lynn nor Donna had ever heard of Paws & Effect™, Heddie Leger, Hero, and Nicole Shumate. One year seven months later Lynn was finishing this book's originals.

Heddie Leger is the Board Advisor of Paws & Effect™.

You can find out more about Paws & Effect™ at www.paws-effect.org. You can E-mail Executive Director Nicole Shumate at nicoleshumate@paws-effect.org.

Dog Scouts of America™

Below is a picture of Hero wearing a neckerchief labeled "Dog Scouts of America™." This was another of Hero's many certifications.

Directly from their website at dogscouts.org, this is what they're all about:

DSA Mission and Vision

"To improve the lives of dogs, their owners, and society through humane education, positive training, and community involvement.

"We envision a future where dogs remain in happy, lifelong homes with responsible owners. In this vision, all dogs are seen as a useful and welcome part of the community, because people take responsibility for socializing, training, containing, and caring for them."

Their mission and vision are exactly what Heddie Leger endorses, lives, and believes in. They are what many responsible dog lovers, owners, breeders, and trainers also believe. Another Paws and Claws Publishing author, Donna Smith Lawrence, also espouses these very important statements.

Hero was a certified Dog Scout of America™. To have earned this, both he and Heddie had to pass the test. The Dog Scout certification is very difficult. Heddie is a ScoutMaster and Evaluator for Dog Scouts of America™.

Hero earned the following Dog Scout badges (given in alphabetical order):

Agility	Community Service	Good Manners
BackPacking	Dog Scout Certification	Hiking
Camping	First Aid	Rally
Carting	Geocaching	Therapy Work

This information is included in this book so that it can be a useful, educational tool for other dog owners. Dog Scouts of America™ is a highly respected, renowned organization.

The Aftermath of the Parkersburg EF5 Tornado in Iowa

On May 25, 2008, a strong super cell developed in northeast Iowa, west of Waterloo, in late afternoon. The first tornado warning was issued at 4:22 P.M. CDT for the Parkersburg area. A large, particularly violent tornado developed shortly thereafter. It started near Aplington in Butler County and then headed toward Parkersburg.

By the time it struck Parkersburg just before 5:00 P.M., it had intensified to EF5 strength and had grown into a large, wedge-shaped tornado. It tore through the southern side of town, which was essentially flattened. Two banks, many homes and businesses, and a high school were destroyed. Parkersburg residential areas were devastated as entire rows of homes were swept away. Hardwood trees were completely denuded and debarked.

Aplington-Parkersburg High School had EF4 damage to its structure. As the tornado exited the east side of town, it struck a golf course and a brand-new subdivision. Many large, well-built homes with anchor bolts were completely swept away. Structural debris from the town was wind-rowed in streaks through area fields, with most of it in small fragments, some no larger than coins.

Afterward the tornado was estimated to have been *about 7/10 of a mile wide* as it struck Parkersburg. Seven people—several of whom were taking shelter in basements—died in town.

The tornado went on to hit New Hartford where two people were killed. Then it passed just north of Waterloo and Cedar Falls. As it approached Dunkerton, it turned and missed the town but grew to up to *1.2 miles wide*. Shortly before it reached Fairbank, it disappeared.

The tornado was later rated an EF5, the first EF5 since the Greensburg, Kansas, one. It reached peak winds of 205 MPH. *Two hundred eighty-eight homes* in Parkersburg were damaged or destroyed, and 88 in and around New Hartford. According to the SPC Storm Reports, 50 tornadoes were reported that day. After the tornado, Governor Chet Culver declared Butler and Black Hawk counties disaster areas. The tornado was the first F5 or EF5 tornado in Iowa since June 13, 1976, and the second deadliest in Iowa since official record-keeping began in 1950. On May 29, 2008, the *Waterloo-Cedar Falls Courier* reported that lightweight debris from Waterloo—photos, check stubs, and greeting cards and business records—had been found in Prairie du Chien, Wisconsin, over 100 miles away.

Heddie Leger and Hero were dispatched by National Animal-Assisted Crisis Response and assigned through the American Red Cross to assist with its mental-health unit for five days. Hero was a certified therapy dog. The duo had taken intensive team training through National Animal-Assisted Crisis Response to assist in the safe recovery and support of those affected by natural and manmade disasters, according to the organization's news release.

National Animal-Assisted Crisis Response teams—which each consist of one handler and one dog—have responded to the World Trade Center attack, Hurricanes Katrina and Rita, and several school shootings.

Heddie and Hero worked with seven other dog-handler teams from Oregon, Iowa, Kansas, Connecticut, and Michigan. They were all unpaid volunteers. They covered their own travel expenses, lodging, and other associated costs.

While the two were in Parkersburg, Hero pulled his cart to deliver water to residents and workers who needed it. They also provided emotional trauma assistance, comfort, and compassion. This was a joint cooperative effort utilizing Hero's and Heddie's expertise in assisting the American Red Cross, FEMA, and the Salvation Army.

In order for any therapy dog to be dispatched, the animal must first be a member of a disaster assistance organization such as National Animal-Assisted Crisis Response (NAACR) or another group due to the extreme emotional trauma that the situation presents. Advanced training is required.

Glossary

chemotherapy *(noun)*—The use of chemical medicines in the treatment of cancer. It often leads to serious side effects, like stomach problems.

clicker training *(noun)*—A way to train puppies and dogs that uses a clicker to let the animal know when it has done the correct behavior. Then the dog is rewarded.

The clicker makes a short click sound that tells the animal when they're doing the right thing. This click sound combined with positive reinforcement is a safe, humane, and effective way to teach the animal a behavior that it is capable of doing. Animals such as dolphins, whales, elephants, seals, rhinoceroses, and other species have been trained with this method.

comparative oncology *(noun)*—The study of tumors that compares and contrasts the appearance of, changes in, and growth of tumors in humans and animals.

dehydrated *(adjective)*—Abnormally lacking in water or body fluids.

lymph nodes *(noun)*—Rounded masses of lymphoid tissue that are found along the lymphatic vessels throughout the body. They filter the flow of *lymph*. Lymph is made of white blood cells but normally no red blood cells. This pale fluid bathes the tissues in the body.

lymphosarcoma *(noun)*—A malignant tumor of lymphoid tissue that tends to spread cancer from one part of the body to another part of the body. It tends to spread freely along the regional drainage for the lymphatic system. It often produces a secondary growth of a malignant tumor.

oncology *(noun)*—The study of tumors.

puppy CPR *(noun)*—Cardiopulmonary resuscitation is a procedure used to try to restore normal breathing after cardiac arrest. It includes clearing the air passages to the lungs, using the mouth-to-mouth method of artificial respiration, and using heart massage by pressing on the chest. It is done by veterinarians and others trained on and certified in puppy CPR.

ReCHAI *(noun)*—Research Center for Human-Animal Interaction. Visit www.rechai.missouri.edu/ to learn more. *Please see page 74.*

rehydrate *(verb)*—To restore fluids to an animal that is dehydrated.

remission *(noun)*—A time period during which cancer is no longer apparent or causing suffering.

Rottweiler *(noun)*—Any of a breed of large, muscular, powerful, black-and-tan, short-haired dogs of German origin. Per the American Kennel Club, they are descendents of Roman drover dogs that drove cattle or sheep.

They are commonly used as guard dogs. Here is a definition from the American Kennel Club: "loyal, loving, confident guardian."

In 1931 the Rottweiler was officially recognized by the American Kennel Club. They state that "Rottweilers love to show off and please their owners." This highly intelligent breed excels at obedience, agility, herding, rally, search and rescue, and carting.

side effect *(noun)*—A secondary and usually bad effect of a drug, such as chemotherapy for cancer.

spleen *(noun)*—A ductless organ located in the left abdominal region near the stomach or intestine of most vertebrates. It does the final destruction of red blood cells. It filters and stores blood. It produces *lymphocytes* that are the cellular elements of lymph and that include the cellular mediators of immunity.

splenectomy *(noun)*—The surgical removal of the spleen.

splenic lymphosarcoma *(noun)*—Lymphosarcoma that is located in the spleen. If not caught early enough in a dog, it can lead the spleen to burst. That can lead to instant death.

stage IV *(noun)*—According to the National Cancer Institute of the National Institutes of Health: "Staging describes the severity of [an animal's] cancer based on the size and/or extent [reach] of the original [primary] tumor and whether or not cancer has spread in the body. Staging is important for several reasons:

- "Staging helps the [veterinarian] plan the appropriate treatment.

- "Cancer stage can be used in estimating [an animal's] prognosis.

- "Knowing the stage of cancer is important in identifying clinical trials that may be a suitable treatment option for a patient.

- "Staging helps health care providers and researchers exchange information about patients; it also gives them a common terminology for evaluating the results of clinical trials and comparing the results of different trials.

"Staging is based on knowledge of the way cancer progresses. Cancer cells grow and divide without control or order, and they do not die when they should. As a result, they often form a mass of tissue called a *tumor*. As a tumor grows, it can invade nearby tissues and organs. Cancer cells can also break away from a tumor and enter the bloodstream or the lymphatic system. By moving through the bloodstream or lymphatic system, cancer cells can spread from the primary site to lymph nodes or to other organs, where they may form new tumors. The spread of cancer is called *metastasis*.

"All cancers are staged when they are first diagnosed. This stage classification, which is typically assigned before treatment, is called the *clinical stage*. A cancer may be further staged after surgery or biopsy, when the extent of the cancer is better known. This stage designation [called the *pathologic stage*] combines the results of the clinical staging with the surgical results.

"A cancer is always referred to by the stage it was given at diagnosis, even if it gets worse or spreads. New information about how a cancer changes over time simply gets added on to the original stage designation. The cancer stage designation doesn't change [even though the cancer itself might] because survival statistics and information on treatment by stage for specific cancer types are based on the original cancer stage at diagnosis."

You can find additional information at the following:

www.cancer.gov/about-cancer/diagnosis-staging/staging/staging-fact-sheet

therapy dog *(noun)*—According to the United States Dog Registry, a therapy dog does the following: A therapy dog "provides affection and comfort to individuals in hospitals, nursing homes, and other facilities."   www.usdogregistry.org

According to Wikipedia, "a *therapy dog* is a dog trained to provide affection and comfort to people in hospitals, retirement homes, nursing homes, schools, hospices, disaster areas, and to people with learning difficulties.

"Therapy dogs are usually not assistance or service dogs, but can be one or both with some organizations."

veterinarian *(noun)*—A person qualified and authorized to practice veterinary medicine.

vet technician *(noun)*—A specialist in the technical details of veterinary medicine.

Where to Find More Information About Topics Related to This Book

ReCHAI (Research Center for Human-Animal Interaction)
MU College of Veterinary Medicine, Clydesdale Hall, Annex #2,
Columbia, MO 65211
www.muserves.missouri.edu/partners/show/643
www.rechai.missouri.edu
rechai@missouri.edu
(573) 882-2266
Rebecca A. Johnson, PhD, RN, FAAN, FNAP—ReCHAI Director
Gretchen Carlisle, RN, MEd, PhD—Postdoctoral Fellow
Dr. Marty Becker, DVM—Adjunct Professor
Dr. Francois Martin, PhD—Adjunct Professor

University of Missouri
www.missouri.edu

University of Missouri–Veterinary Medical Teaching Hospital
Clydesdale Hall, 900 East Campus Drive, Columbia, MO 65211
www.vmth.missouri.edu
Administration: (573) 882-7821
Small Animal: (573) 882-7821
Equine: (573) 882-3513
Food Animal: (573) 882-6857

Liberty Public Schools, Liberty, Missouri
www.liberty.k12.mo.us

Mo-Kan Pet Partners
www.mo-kanpetpartners.org

The PawZone!
PO Box 872, Liberty, MO 64068
www.thepawzone.com/
pawzone@yahoo.com
(816) 820-5829

Paws & Effect™—Charitable, Nonprofit Organization
www.paws-effect.org/
nicoleshumate@paws-effect.org
(515) 822-5285
www.facebook.com/PawsEffectOrg
The founder of Paws & Effect™: Nicole Shumate—Executive Director
The Board Advisor of Paws & Effect™: Heddie Leger

We all need a little help from our friends.

Heddie Leger would like to give special recognition to the Missouri Alliance for Animal Legislation. They work tirelessly with legislators in Missouri to pass laws to protect animals and to fight breed-specific legislation, which is one of the biggest issues that she taught with Hero. You can find out more about them at the following: www.maal.org

The End

www.ingramcontent.com/pod-product-compliance
Lightning Source LLC
LaVergne TN
LVHW070834080426

835508LV00031B/3460